Out of the Fire:
Surviving Flight 17K
The Life Story of
Eugene Casey

Out of the Fire: Surviving Flight 17K The Life Story of Eugene Casey

Peggy Moffitt

Copyright © 2017 by Peggy Moffitt.

ISBN: Softcover   978-1-5434-3710-2
          eBook   978-1-5434-3709-6

All rights reserved. No part of this book may be reproduced or transmitted in any form or by any means, electronic or mechanical, including photocopying, recording, or by any information storage and retrieval system, without permission in writing from the copyright owner.

Any people depicted in stock imagery provided by Thinkstock are models, and such images are being used for illustrative purposes only.
Certain stock imagery © Thinkstock.

Print information available on the last page.

Rev. date: 08/10/2017

To order additional copies of this book, contact:
Xlibris
1-888-795-4274
www.Xlibris.com
Orders@Xlibris.com
763272

CONTENTS

Dedication vii

Author's Note 1

The Early Years 3

The Crash 25

Marriage and Children 45

Being a Police Officer 49

Happily Ever After 57

Acknowledgements, Credits, and References 61

Dedication

To those who perished and to those who miraculously survived.

Those who died	**Survivors**	
W. P. Anderson	James Adams	Robert Oberg
P. V. Black	Eugene Casey	John Predergast
H. L. Brown	Richard Coon	William Queen
Vincent E. Borders	Earl Edinger	Roger Ricker
Robert J. Caruth	Robert Fischer	Felix St. Louis
J. J. Clersiak	Theodore Gostinger	Dale Shewmake
T. C. Dillo	Rhiner Groendyk	Joseph Simon
H. B. Duncan	Michele Guerrera	Eugene Smith
F. J. Ernst	Fred Hall	James Smith
R. F. Hayes	James Harrison	Raymond Stalter
T. A. Jackson	Robert Holland	Robert Stuart
A. Kaukes	Frederick Hudson	Peter Tamburin
Edward McGrath	John Jamison	Hiram Thomas
H. Mangino, Jr.	Donald Johnson	John Thomas
J. K. Moore	William Johnson	Everett Trainor
R. E. Norden	David Kent	Ken Uppstrom
James Parker	Reginald Layoff, Jr.	Thomas Van Horn
J. A. Peterson	Elbert Leatherman	Hugo Weiss
A. M. Roehling	Charles Lenhart	Robert Wescott
D. Russell, Jr.	James McDevitt	
N. T. Seeley	William McDougall	
C. J. Shelton	Virginia McGrath	
R. E. Thornton	Richard McGrath	
A. P. Truitt	Tom McGrath	
Donald G. Tuma	Mary McGrath	
V. J. "Tiger" Tylinski	Andrew Malinarko	
W. W. Wojick	Ladislas Marics	
Raymond Mero		

Author's Note

My deepest gratitude to Mr. Casey and his fellow soldiers
for their service to our country.
Thank you for your patience during this long project,
for your dedication, encouragement, and confidence in me to
document your extraordinary life. I hope I did a good job.

To my husband, Gary, thank you for your love and support
and to those who still believe in me.
In the distance and silence, my heart holds you.

Peace and love,
Peggy A. Moffitt

The Early Years

"After sixty years, there is so much about the plane crash I vividly remember, as if it was yesterday," Gene said. With pen and pads of yellow-lined paper, he carefully writes about his life from his youth to present day. He may stop to ponder what he chooses to document, but he perseveres to record his memories with careful consideration. One memory leads to another and faded details reemerge for Gene's personal reflection. He may smile, maybe chuckle a time or two, or perhaps he may need to wipe the tears from his eyes in quiet contemplation. He may stop to rest his hand and look out of the window of his Florida home to glimpse the innocent birds and wind in the trees. Soon the pages become a powerful collection of priceless letters. These personal recollections come from a life filled with good and bad, adventure and duty. He is humble and epitomizes the meaning of *survivor*.

Gene is a United States Army Veteran, former Chicago police officer, successful business man, loving husband, and a proud father and grandfather. All of this after nearly being killed in a blazing plane crash.

Born in Chicago on Friday, June 26, 1936, Eugene "Gene" Frank Casey was one of eighteen children born to John Patrick Casey. Fourteen children by his first wife, Martha, and four by his mother, Anna, his second wife. "My father was a very disciplined, strict, hard man," Gene said. "He had a great business sense and was physically strong. He worked 8:00 a.m. to 5:00 p.m. in Chicago where he owned a bank and several commercial and residential apartment buildings." Away from the hectic city, Gene's father enjoyed the country. "His hobby was an eighty-acre piece of property on Bass Lake, outside of Knox, Indiana," Gene said. "After being a widower for many years, he met my mother in the little town of Knox, Indiana, close to Bass Lake. She was working in her family's plumbing business. During the summer, he worked on the farm and occasionally would go to Chicago for a few days leaving my mom and us boys behind. Once in a while, in the winter, he would go during the weekends. Sometimes we would all go with him. He was always dressed in a long-sleeved white shirt, a straw hat, and old suit pants. Sometimes he wore work pants, but he always wore suspenders."

"He could be funny," Gene said as he reflects on his father's dominant personality, "but he was never quiet and always stern. He had no hobbies because he worked and farmed. "Our relationship was quite strained," Gene said. "He took me to one movie, *The Biscuit Eater*."

"On Sunday, June 4, 1950, I was at St. Joseph's Military Academy in La Grange, Illinois. The school was hosting its annual fund-raising carnival. I was excited because my mother was coming for the day. Unfortunately, she didn't come and she sent my nephew, Richard Casey and my niece, Mary Lou Kockleman. They said my father was in a very serious accident on the farm and was in the Starke County Hospital in Knox, Indiana. My mother also told them not to reveal too much so as not to upset me."

"On the 29th of May, my dad was alone at our farm. He was seventy-eight years old and cutting brush with a self-propelled mower that had a large rotating blade on the front. Apparently, he walked in front of it to clear obstacles and debris before taking the machine out of gear or the machine vibrated itself back into gear. It crept up on him and the blade cut through his shoe, breaking three bones in his foot and breaking a finger. He needed nineteen stitches in his knees."

"My dad said that our dog, Susie, a mixed Shepherd, came to him sensing his distress. He held on to her collar and she pulled him as he crawled as best as possible to the house, where he managed to get inside and call for help. He never fully recovered from the accident, but he did get around fairly well and was able to drive, although my mother did most of the driving from then on."

"I thought he got along very well, seeing his age and his devastating injuries. He used a crutch to get around on the farm. He built a large replica of a wheelchair with car tires. He managed to scoot around some, but if any of us where there we would push him out into the gardens so he could get up to rake and hoe. My dad was very tough. He considered the accident nothing more than an inconvenience. We never thought he was in trouble."

Gene pauses as he remembers his dear mother, Anna. "She was a very gregarious, loving person," Gene said fondly. "She was as hard a worker as my dad, whether it be housekeeping, helping at my dad's office, working on the farm canning all night, or raising us four boys, Dan, Tom, Mike, and I."

"They both were very religious and never missed Sunday mass," he said. "My mother would often walk to daily mass in Chicago. She was kind and loving to everyone and was my father's caregiver until he passed. After that, she helped others and often drove folks around to places they needed to go. My parents didn't have hobbies per se except that Mom played golf before marrying my dad and was an avid pinochle player, as were all of us. Sometimes the games were all-nighters. Dad played pinochle in my early days."

Gene had thirteen brothers and four sisters from his father's two marriages. Raised on the south side of the Windy City, Gene attended St. Dorothy's Grammar School from first to sixth grade, St. Joseph's Military Academy from seventh to eight grade, and attended St. Rita High School. The Korean War Armistice Agreement was signed on July 27, 1953 and nine days later at the tender age of seventeen, Gene decided to join the Army.

"I joined because I wanted the experience," he said, "to get out of Chicago and away from the environment I had created; hanging out at a bowling alley, not getting along at home, not able to hold a job, wanting to play all the time, no discipline. Yet, I never was in any kind of trouble. Going into the Army was the best thing I ever did. My parents thought it was a good idea and signed for me to enter right after my seventeenth birthday. I'm sure it relieved them of a lot of worry of where I was and what I was doing."

"Going to St. Joseph's Military Academy did not have any influence on my decision to join the Army," he said, "except for the fact that I enjoyed the extra freedom of being away from home." The school was operated by Roman Catholic nuns, Sisters of St. Joseph, in La Grange Park, a suburb west of Chicago. "I took two streetcars and the Burlington Zephyr to get there," he said. "I caught the Zephyr at a small stop above 18th and south Western Avenue. I walked about a mile after getting off the train in La Grange."

Military service runs in Gene's family. "My mother's dad served in the Spanish American War," Gene explained. "His dad and his dad's brother served in the Civil War." Gene was the fifth child in his family to enter the military. His three older brothers, Leonard, Harry, and Howard, honorably served their country; Leonard in World War I, Harry and Howard in World War II. "Michael was the eighteenth child," Gene said. "He was in the Air Force during the Vietnam War as an observer stationed in Pakistan at the same base American pilot Francis Gary Powers flew out of. Leonard was born on December 16, 1897, the oldest of eighteen children. I know little about his service other than he was on a destroyer ship in the Mediterranean Sea and spent some time in Egypt. He had three children, all of whom are deceased."

"Harry was single and never drove," he said. "He was in World War II. His job was to dig up or dig out unexploded artillery shells, bombs, etc. He never told me this himself, but that is what the family said. I first remember him in the early 1940's, in uniform. When he left the service, he went to work at a railroad shipping and receiving complex. He had problems with gout most of his life. He did like his beer and pinochle."

"Starting in the late 1950's and through the 60's," Gene continued, "I drove Harry to most family functions. He loved to play pinochle, as we all did, so I would always take him to Bass Lake for all-night laughing pinochle games, all day too. He was a very nice, friendly man whom I loved very much. He really enjoyed his life, lonely as it may have seemed."

Gene fondly remembers his brother Howard, who was born on October 13, 1914. "He was the thirteenth child of my dad's first marriage," he said. "I don't know why I know his face as I have no memory of meeting him before 1944. Before being drafted on December 8, 1943, Howard was listed as secretary of my dad's bank. In 1944, Howard came by our home with his wife, Katherine, and their children, Howie and Kathy, while he was on leave before being deployed to Germany. He was in uniform. They had taken the old double-decker bus on South Park, got off at 78th Street, and walked the four blocks to our home. I remember him saying that Howie had gotten one of his ribbons loose and must have dropped it on the bus.

I took a picture of the four of them on our front steps with a Sears camera I got for Christmas. That was, at least to my memory, the first time I saw him in person. As it turned out, it was the last."

"On December 1, 1944, he was killed near Luxembourg. My dad said he had heard they were running from tree to tree when Howard was killed. Residents in the area retrieved their bodies and buried them in their own little makeshift cemeteries. They took their personal effects and displayed them in curio cabinets. They also notified the soldiers' families. I believe it was in December."

Often the processes we must endure are painful. Doing the right thing for a loved one, or simply because it's the nature of propriety in the name of life and death, can be a long grueling ordeal.

"Around that time," Gene continues, "Holy Sepulchre Catholic Cemetery in Alsip, Illinois was developing a previously undeveloped part of their large cemetery, which was to be dedicated to war heroes. My dad bought a thirty-one-plot parcel and ordered a huge marble cross from Italy, which was to be cut from one piece of marble, and cost $15,000. On the way to America the ship was in a major storm and the cross was cracked so another one was ordered which made it to the cemetery in one piece."

"My mother had aunts and uncles who lived in the Luxembourg area so my dad sent my mother there to retrieve Howard's remains so that he would be buried in the new part of Holy Sepulchre. He sent a $500.00 check for the family who rescued Howard's remains and told them they could keep his personal effects as part of their little war museum."

Grief causes us to seek comfort in many ways. How lovely it might be if the warmth of our beds magically transformed into huge hands to cradle us while we weep. Grieving the loss of her brother, Gene's sister, Irma, took Howard's death very hard. "She laid in her bed crying for more than one day," Gene said. "She then took me to his wife Kathryn's apartment above a bungalow at 6938 South Park Avenue in Chicago. Everyone was sad…my dad was very quiet."

During war, it was common to see service banners hanging in the windows of homes across America. Families who had a relative serving their country would hang a service flag in honor of their loved one. "The shrine in our home had flags in the front window," Gene said, "one for Harry and one for Howard. When there was a death, the flag changed from a blue star to a gold star."

"Howard's body was shipped back and was the first to be buried in the new cemetery parcel. His mother, Martha, was later moved from her resting place and buried in the plot. My dad was buried later next to her and still later my mother on the other side of my dad. Kathryn died in Michigan in 2015 at the age of ninety-three. Both children also live in Michigan."

After his parents signed the paperwork allowing Gene to enter the Army, Gene said his goodbyes and was sent to Camp Crowder, south of Neosho, Missouri, for indoctrination. Next, he went to Fort Riley, Kansas for sixteen weeks of heavy weapons training, then to Fort Benning, Georgia for airborne training and then on to Fort Lee, Virginia for parachute rigging, assigned to the Quartermaster Corps.

Although Gene was young with his life ahead of him, his freedom and independence didn't get the best of him. "I did not find my new amount of freedom overwhelming whatsoever," he said. "Military life is very confining with all its rules and regulations. There is no freedom, just regimental control."

In June of 1954, Gene sailed to Korea where he stayed for sixteen months. "I don't recall the name of the ship," he said, "but we had to anchor at sea because of an outbreak of spinal meningitis. Quarantine flags were raised and the ship was at rest until the disease was in check."

"In Korea, I served in the 7th, 2nd, and 24th Infantry Divisions," he said. "I went to Korea as an Army Airborne Rigger. There was no need for them so I was assigned to the 2nd Infantry Division at Chorwon Valley as a cook in training. Later I was assigned to the 7th Infantry Division again at Chorwon Valley, in a heavy mortar company. We were assigned to the DMZ (Demilitarized Zone), and later to Uijpngbu. When the 7th rotated home, I was once again reassigned to the 24th Division at Chorwon Valley as a cook and baker. I was trained by a soldier whose parents owned a bakery in the States. He was a very religious man. I enjoyed cooking and baking," Gene said. "I was a pretty good cook and baker with what I had to work with in the field. My mom would send me vanilla extract, which was not available locally. I was later assigned with the 24th to Munsan Ni, an administrative division of Paju-si, Gyeonggi-do, on the south bank of the Imjin River in South Korea. I rotated home from that area in 1955."

During times of war, it's common for celebrities, (singers, actors and comedians), to visit American troops to lift their morale. "One time I was assigned to the officer's mess hall where Debbie Reynolds and Marilyn Monroe both ate," he said. "I remember Debbie being asked about Eddie Fisher; she refused to answer." Entertainers Eddie Fisher and Debbie Reynolds were married from 1955-1959 until he left Debbie to marry her best friend, actress Elizabeth Taylor. It was one of the biggest celebrity scandals at the time. "I did not meet the stars and did not have any interest in photographs or meeting them," he said. "That was only for the higher ups."

One particular person was on Gene's mind while he was thousands of miles from home. Her name was Mary Lou Young. "Mary Lou and

I lived two streetcars and a train ride apart," he explained. "I lived in Chicago and she lived in La Grange. We met while I was going to St. Joseph's Military Academy. She attended Our Lady of Bethlehem Girls School. The schools adjoined one another. We didn't see each other often, except periodically when I was assigned as an altar boy. Her family was very religious and said the rosary each evening as a family on their knees. We did the same in our home. When I would pick her up to go to her friends or to just walk or go to a show, I always joined her family in praying their rosaries. We wrote each other the whole three years I was in the service. She picked me up at the railroad station on Christmas Eve in 1955, my first trip home in two years. That's when she hugged me for the first time. She dropped me off at home, met my mom, then left without coming inside. In January of 1956, we went on a date to the drive-in. I never saw her again after that night. I had the opinion her parents did not like me."

"Religion is a very large part of my life," he said. "I am Catholic and I like to believe I'm a good Catholic. Prayer, I believe, has always helped me. I pray over and for everything. I feel my prayers, for the most part, are always answered."

"Before I left Korea I went to mass and communion and prayed for my trip," he said. "I also went to mass and communion twice aboard the ship. I dreamt I was in an airplane crash one night, but ignored it as a warning and prayed all would be all right. As it turned out, all *was* not all right. I carried a small pouch my mom gave me all the time with a rosary, a medal, and a small prayer book, which survived the crash in my pocket."

"We left Korea in late October of 1955 on a Merchant Marine ship, the General R. L. Howze. It was the last regular troopship bringing servicemen home from Korea. We were the last troopship to dock in Tacoma, Washington on November 17th, 1955. We never left the port of embarkation due to the bad weather. We docked one morning and flew out that night."

A lot happens in one day. As the days add up, every year is packed with significant events that become history; 1955 was no exception. That year the U.S. performed nuclear tests in Nevada and the Pacific Ocean. President Dwight D. Eisenhower was the first president to hold a televised news conference. He raised the minimum wage from $0.75 to $1.00 an hour. *The Millionaire* and the *Lawrence Welk Show* premiered. Singer Carl Perkins recorded *Blue Suede Shoes*. Ray Kroc opened his first fast food restaurant, McDonalds, in Des Plaines, Illinois. Disneyland opened in Anaheim, California. School integration was ordered by the Supreme Court. Civil rights activist Rosa Parks was arrested for refusing to give up her seat to a white passenger on a city bus in Montgomery, Alabama. Congress ordered "*In God We Trust*" to be engraved on all coins. Singer and cultural icon Elvis Presley made his first television appearance. The world lost theoretical physicist Albert Einstein and actor James Dean.

JOHN CASEY WITH 13 OF HIS 18 CHILDREN. GENE IS THE BABY, THE FIRST OF FOUR CHILDREN BORN TO JOHN AND ANNA CASEY.

A DRAWING OF JOHN CASEY'S BANK IN CHICAGO

**GENE'S PARENTS:
JOHN "JP" AND ANNA CASEY IN 1934.**

YOUNG MOM

ANNA CASEY

About 1946-1948

Dan   Mike   Tom   Gene

GENE, YOUNG CADET

GENE WITH HIS MOTHER

**JOHN CASEY BEFORE THE ACCIDENT.
MOM'S SISTER ON THE RIGHT, HER AUNT ON THE LEFT.**

GENE CASEY'S MOTHER (LEFT), SISTER (RIGHT), UNIDENTIFIED MAN (CENTER)

CASEY FAMILY SUMMER HOME IN BASS LAKE, INDIANA.

CHATHAM BOWL LATER BECAME SOUTH PARK LANES, THEN KING BOWL

The Crash

Perhaps each of us can choose one day in our existence that truly lives in infamy. Aviation records state that around the world on November 17, 1955 there were one hundred forty-four plane crashes. Gene was on one of those planes. Back in Chicago on that memorable day the dreary, winter temperature was 33° F. Former Illinois Governor Adlai Stevenson II announced his campaign for the Democratic Presidential nomination. The Chicago Bears midseason record was five and three.

"I do remember the walk to the airport in the snow during an almost blinding blizzard," he said "but I have no idea how far I walked. The walk took place at night, I would say between 8:00 and 11:00p.m. I bought a life insurance policy for sixty thousand dollars from a machine and mailed it to my mother. I called her to let her know I was back in the States and I would be flying out later that night. She was not aware that I had been rotated out of Korea. There were no buses or taxis running. My duffle bag was too heavy to shoulder that far or I was too lazy so I dragged it behind me. I had another small suitcase which I carried."

Many soldiers were trying to get home to their loved ones for Thanksgiving and Christmas. "I do not remember making the walk with anyone in particular. There were a lot of us and we were spread out walking down the middle of the street, as there was no traffic whatsoever. I remember crossing a bridge over water or something, an older bridge with lots of cross beams."

"We bought our tickets from the Army at the port where we arrived because the Army had chartered the plane. I looked out of the airport windows and watched the blowing snow and men on our plane's wings trying to keep the accumulating snow brushed off. I saw our two pilots sitting at the bar wearing sunglasses. They told me it was so their eyes would become accustomed to the dark."

Operated by Peninsula Air Transport, flight 17K was bound for Billings, Montana, then Chicago, Illinois, and Newark, New Jersey. Seventy-four people were on board the Douglas DC-4, seventy passengers and four crewmembers. Twenty-eight lost their lives due to maintenance errors.

"The plane the Army chartered was a mess from the git go. The plane did not have a tail wheel. We were welcomed on the plane by a steward. He had forgot to put the tail bar under the tail until they got the weight distributed. We loaded from the back of the plane in front of the tail, almost exactly from where I escaped. The plane squatted and we had to unload so it would right itself and have the room for the bar to be installed. We then loaded. I sat up front behind a mother and three children so I could watch the pilots, but changed my mind at the last minute. I took an aisle seat, the third of three, next to an emergency exit door, which was across from the door I had entered."

"When we started towards the runway, there was a lot of banging coming from the rear of the plane. The plane went back to the terminal, where the steward exited the plane to retrieve the pole he had installed to prop up the tail while we were loading. Having already dreamt about a plane crash on the ship from Korea, I should have gotten off right then and there".

"I sat next to and on the right of Corporal James Parker, a buddy from Korea who lived ten blocks from me in Chicago. He was decapitated by the same piece of metal that injured me. He and I lived in the same neighborhood and planned on hanging around together."

"When the plane was airborne," Gene explained, "an engine on the right wing exploded in flames and revved up. The pilot gave full power, but to no avail. We just weren't high enough, but still climbing. The tail hit the ground and bounced back up high enough for us to clear a highway and headed for a large tree on the left side. The highway was well lit and there was a car going under us from my left to the right. The night was beautiful in that it was snowing, the streetlights had halos around them and the car lights cast a glow. It could have been on a Christmas card."

"After the tail hit the ground and we were airborne again, I heard three of the four engines roaring. I remember thinking that the guys at my old hangout, the Chatham Bowling Alley, were never going to believe that I crashed and bounced up and was airborne again. I really thought we'd stay up. When we hit the ground again, I watched the left wing crumple back toward the fuselage. When we slapped the ground the second time, it was so hard I felt like the downward impact to my body was crushing me. That second and final slap on the ground snapped the tail section off and I thought my back was broken. I guess I passed out from the pain. Before I passed out, I remembered seeing seats with people in them sailing through the air on the right side of the fuselage, not all the seats, mind you, about eleven would be my guess. I was in the tail section at the front of where it snapped off. The tree the plane hit was a very large elm, planted there on Des Moines Memorial Drive in honor of World War I veterans. I was also told that as of 2012 the ground that was burned the most from the plane fire is still black and barren."

"After the crash, I grabbed a GI who was stumbling around and looked like he may fall. I directed him out where the tail broke off. Another GI, who was African American, was sitting on the floor distressed because he couldn't get up. In the hospital, they told me part of his butt was burned off. He said that he couldn't get up and to please help him. I reached for him and he grabbed my arms. Being burned, the skin was slippery. Some slid off in his hands. I was afraid if I fell or he pulled me down, I wouldn't be able to get up. I leaned over, he wrapped an arm around my neck, and as I stood up I pulled him to his feet. Once he was on his feet he stumbled, but with my arm around him he was fine."

"We were not feeling severe pain because it was so darn cold. We got behind a garage, stopped, looked back and what was left of the plane exploded in a ball of fire. With my arm wrapped around him, I guided us to a house, knocked on the front door and we were welcomed inside. The other GI was taken to the kitchen where more GI's had already gathered."

"The lady who let us in screamed when she saw me. She made me lay down on the living room floor. I was shaking so bad it hurt. Another woman, a young Asian lady, tried to help me by trying to hold me still and covered me with blankets, which seemed to worsen the pain. The lady that let us in went to the front door and screamed for help. A man came and told her they had no more room in their ambulance, but that they would come back. She brought him to me and after he saw me he went back to the front door and yelled to the other medics to unload the ambulance and bring a stretcher."

"By now I was screaming in pain as the house was quite warm. I screamed from then on. In the hospital, I begged to be knocked out with a sedative. The nurse told me repeatedly that they were giving me everything they could and to try to relax. Then I finally passed out. At first I was wrapped from head to toe in bandages with only a breathing hole for my mouth and nose and holes for my eyes. The nurse who stayed with me in a pitched black room asked me if I smoked. I told her 'yes'. She lit up a cigarette and blew the smoke into the hole over my mouth."

"Then a reporter from the *Seattle Times* newspaper came into my room and asked if I would talk to him about the crash. In return, he would call my mother. He called her and the call ran into her calling me, I believe, in Atlanta, Georgia. Her first words to me were, *'what did you do now?'*"

"My mother later told me that before she received the first notification of the accident, possibly a telegram, she woke up about 3:30 a.m. and woke my dad up. She told him she thought something bad had happened to me. She said she was dreaming that her mom, deceased eleven years, and I were arguing in the dining room downstairs. Her mom pushed me and I fell against the radiator and split open the left side of my head. My head was split open over my left ear causing a fractured skull. My dad then said he was also dreaming about me. He said in his dream we were at our home in Bass Lake and he was in the field working when he heard me screaming. He looked toward the house and I was standing in the doorway screaming, completely on fire. At this time, they both got up and turned the radio on for the news."

"In the hospital, the next day I was visited by an Army Major, who returned my fare in cash in a brown pay-like envelope. I think it was $54.00 and change. He was the same Major who later brought the second solider I rescued to visit me in a wheelchair because the soldier wanted to thank me for saving his life. I thought I could get up to shake his hand, but when I put my weight on my legs, the blisters under the cotton bandages popped open and watery fluid sprayed on to the floor. The pressure of standing forced some of the liquid out through the bandages around my thighs."

"The Major said that if my bubble brass had not deflected the piece of the wing, it would have gone through me. As it was, the crushed clavicle had splintered in that area, trapping or being close to a main artery, making it necessary to be careful until it healed as not to let any splintered bone pierce the artery."

"The Major told me I was being put in for the Soldiers Medal for my bravery. He also confirmed that I had helped another soldier before I picked this soldier up. I never got the medal for reasons unknown, which I have pursued as late as 2017, partially because they say my records were lost in a fire…how ironic."

Gene sustained burns on his head, face, neck, hands, legs, and genital area. "A doctor told me I had burns over twenty percent of my body, a crushed clavicle and a fractured skull. My left ear was burned, causing the ear canal passage to narrow and the ear drum to thicken. He said the Army was transferring me to Brooke Army Medical Center, (BAMC), in San Antonia, Texas for burn research. He said that whatever slammed into my clavicle was stopped by something else that prevented it from piercing through me. Later he figured out it was my bubble brass that deflected the piece of the wing."

"I was flown alone to BAMC the next day on a large two-engine medical ambulance and had my bandages removed when I arrived. My doctor, Major John A. Moncrief, later became a colonel for his successful work in burn injuries. They put me under a bacteria-controlled tent to keep the bed sheets from coming in contact with the burns. Under the tent was a fan that blew on me around the clock. Scabs quickly formed and nurses would use scissors and tweezers to peel and cut them off. Some of the scabs were as big as dinner plates. My back was also injured. I had to lay flat for two weeks with sandbags under me. I was sent home for twelve days on Christmas Eve. Later, I was sent home for two 30-day medical leaves. In March of 1956 I was sent to Fort Riley, Kansas where I was a cook and was discharged in October."

"Since the crash, I have never had any strange experiences, dreams, or visions from it. It has never bothered me at all. The Veterans Administration wanted to treat me for any mental trauma from the airplane crash that I might have harbored, but they dismissed me and were sure there was no trauma."

"Many years after the crash, I heard from a GI I did not know who came back from Korea on the same ship as I did. Because of the bad weather, he cancelled his flight on my plane, took a hotel room for the night, and caught a train the next day. The other man I heard from lived in the neighborhood where the plane crashed. He saw the plane go over the highway. He went to the crash site and backed his '49 Ford into a driveway across the street from the house that took me in, and he watched the burning, the explosions, and heard the screaming. He was nineteen at the time and later bought that house and lives there today. He said the people in the neighborhood still talk about that fateful night. How about that? We wrote a couple of times and called each other twice. I think talking to him helped me make my decision to have my story written. It's funny how vivid the memories are after all this time."

"My duffle bag did not make the flight because of weight restrictions. It caught up with me at Brooke Army Medical Center. It had all my clothes in it plus a lady's watch I had bought for Mary Lou. When I got home for Christmas Eve in 1955, I gave it to my mother. My most important bag, the carry-on, was lost. It had all my pictures and mementoes. I presume it was lost or found and kept, not knowing who it belonged to."

One would think that such a traumatic event would significantly change a person's behavior or outlook on life, but it didn't for Gene. "The plane crash gave me no extra skills, intuition, knowledge, or inner strength to be a successful anything," he said. "It showed me how tough the body is, and that you can survive a horrific incident. Though I do not fly anymore because of the accident, I have flown in the past although the fear of losing my life is pretty much nil, but why tempt fate?"

Understandably, the human body can take only so much abuse. "Because of my multiple burns and back injuries," he said, "there are things I can no longer do because of the physical nature of it, and my delicate skin over time prohibits me now from being in the sun, like tennis and golf."

GENE IN 1953

47 SURVIVE IN AIR-LINER CRASH WHICH KILLED 27 NEAR RIVERTON

SEATTLE, WASHINGTON, FRIDAY, NOVEMBER 18, 1955

FLIGHT'S END: Rescuers removed the body of one of the 27 persons who died early today when this nonscheduled DC-4 air liner cashed into the back yard of a home at 12010 Des Moines Way. Another stretcher crew at right returnded to the smoldering wreckage to remove other victims. Forty-seven persons survived. The plane crashed shortly after taking off from Boeing Field. - Times photo by George Carkonen.

The Seattle Times
FRIDAY, NOVEMBER 18, 1955.

CRASH SCENE: The broken line, beginning at the upper right corner of this aerial photo, shows the course of the ill-fated air liner which crashed and burned in the Boulevard Park District last night. Numbered markers indicate (1) where the craft sheared off the top of a tree, (2) felled a utility pole, (3) demolished a garage and grazed a corner of the home of Mr. and Mrs. Sam Montgomery, 1829 S. 120th St., and (4) crashed and exploded in the yard of Mr. and Mrs. Colin F. Dearing. The tail section is just to the right of (4) - A. P. photo.

The Seattle Times
FRIDAY, NOVEMBER 18, 1955

Craft Carrying G. I.'s Hits House; Failure Of Engine Held to Blame

Two full pages of plane-wreck pictures, Pages 12 and 13. Other photos and details, Pages 2, 7, 23.

In a miraculous mass escape, 47 persons, including three children, survived the crash of a nonscheduled DC-4 last midnight in a Boulevard Park back yard, near Riverton, two and a half miles south of Boeing Field.

At least 25 soldiers, who were flying home for Thanksgiving, and two other persons were killed.

The four-engined Peninsular Air Transport plane pancaked into a snow-covered field behind the home of Colin F. Dearing, Sr., 12010 Des Moines Way, two minutes after it took off from Boeing Field for the East. Engine failure was believed the cause of the crash.

The plane caught fire and exploded, spewing flames over the Dearing house. Mrs. Dearing and her five children escaped without injury.

As the flames roared through the transport, the passengers and crew jumped, stumbled, fell or were carried through huge holes in the fuselage.

Those who died were trapped in the flaming cabin.

The Civil Aeronautics Board is conducting a hearing in Miami on complaints that Peninsular has overloaded its planes and overworked its pilots. (See Page 2 for details.)

Returning Soldiers Chartered Plane

The plane was chartered by 65 soldiers who returned from Korea yesterday morning on Navy transport Gen. R. L. Howze.

Besides a three-man crew, Edward McGrath, a newly hired Peninsular pilot, was aboard the plane with his wife and three children, moving from Oakland to Miami.

Mrs. McGrath and the children, Mary Ellen, 4; Tommy, 5, and Richard, 8, survived with hardly a scratch. McGrath was killed.

The crew members—William McDougall, pilot; Fred Hall, co-pilot, both of Miami, and James O. Adams, steward, Hialeah, Fla.—were injured.

At least five soldiers were in serious condition today and others were recovering from burns. Several, however, suffered only slight bruises.

SEATTLE DAILY TIME, PAGE 1 STORY, NOVEMBER 18, 1955

Snow Falling but Visibility Good

Light snow was falling as McDougall piloted the plane down the icy runway in a southeasterly direction. Visibility was seven miles. A layer of broken clouds hung at an altitude of 1,600 feet.

As McDougall banked the plane for a right turn over the Duwamish River after taking off, survivors said an engine sputtered, roared, sputtered, caught for a final moment and then began missing badly.

The plane began losing altitude and the houses and trees of the Riverton area loomed ahead.

The plane sheared a tree on the north side of South 120th Street near Des Moines Way, toppled a power pole across the street and crashed into a cottonwood tree in the Dearings' yard after smashing a shop and garage belonging to the Dearings' neighbor, Sam Montgomery, 1829 S. 120th St. (See Page 23 for aerial photo-map of crash scene.)

The right wing of the plane grazed Montgomery's house. The left wing was ripped loose

(See Page 12, Column 1.)

(Continued From Page One)

against an oak tree in the Dearings' yard.

Fuel Tank Explodes

As the plane careened over the snow, the tail twisted off, leaving a large hole in the rear of the cabin. It was through this hole that most of the survivors escaped.

The plane traveled only about 100 yards after striking the first tree.

Fire spread quickly through the cabin. Many of the survivors broke through flames to safety. Minutes after the crash a fuel tank exploded, dooming those still in the wreckage.

"It was a miracle, that's what—just a miracle anyone lived through the crash," said E. J. Rice, 1865 S. 120th St.

SEATTLE DAILY TIMES, PAGE 1 STORY, NOVEMBER 18, 1955, CONTINUED

Rice was walking near the scene as the crippled plane roared earthward. He was on his way to help a neighbor whose home was being flooded by water from broken pipes.

"The plane's engines were popping and sputtering and that pilot knew he was going to crash," Rice said. "It looked as though he was fighting to reach a little clear space among the houses."

"When I got there a couple of soldiers were wandering around. I did what I could to help them, and then helped some of the others."

Other neighbors echoed Rice's awe. Another part of the "miracle" they said, was that the plane crashed, broke apart and burst into towering flames without damaging any of the houses, except the Dearings' and Montgomerys', clustered on the slope of the low hill.

The neighbors opened their homes to the survivors and gave them first aid, coffee and blankets until ambulances arrived.

Ambulances, volunteer firemen, police, sheriffs' deputies and state patrolmen were slowed by snowy roads in reaching the scene. When they arrived, some survivors huddled in nearby homes. Others wandered dazed along the roads.

The wreck became a scene of horror.

Coroner's deputies, firemen and other searchers probed the smoking wreckage for bodies. Spectators looked on in awed silence as the bodies were carried past them.

A blackened, flame-seared tree stood at the rear of the Dearing home like a macabre sentinel watching over the rescue workers.

Although the crash occurred outside the city, members of the Police Department were there in force to assist.

The dead were taken to the King County morgue. Positive identification proceeded slowly as Army officers checked Army dental records. The F. B. I. assisted in attempting to identify the dead through fingerprints.

C. A. B. Official at Scene

Joseph P. Adams, a former Seattle lawyer who is vice chairman of the Civil Aeronautics Board, went to the scene. Adams, here to inspect the Boeing 707 Jet Stratoliner, was notified of the crash while at a hotel.

After conferring with Frank K. McKlveen, a representative of the Bureau of Safety Investigation, Adams called the C. A. B. in Washington to have additional personnel assigned to investigate the crash.

The plane was scheduled to land in Billings, Mont., Chicago and Newark.

The Boeing Field control tower had no radio contact with McDougall after clearing the plane for take-off.

McDougall is a major in the Air Force Reserves. He was a ferry pilot in the Second World War and served with the Strategic Air Command in Alaska. He declined to discuss the accident.

Hall, the co-pilot, was a marine during the Second World War.

SEATTLE DAILY TIMES, PAGE 1 STORY, NOVEMBER 18, 1955, CONTINUED

The Seattle Times
FRIDAY, NOVEMBER 18, 1955.

Bandaged Survivor Just Wants to See His Girl

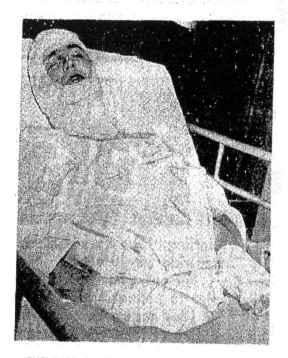

SURVIVOR: Swathed in bandages, Eugene Casey, Chicago, a survivor of the Riverton crash, looked up from his bed in Standring Memorial Hospital to recount details of the mishap. Physicians said Casey, 19, is in satisfactory condition.

The Seattle Times
FRIDAY, NOVEMBER 18, 1955.

Bandaged Survivor Just Wants to See His Girl

"I don't know if she'll have me now," Eugene Casey, 19, Chicago, a soldier-survivor of the DC-4 chartered air liner that crashed near Riverton last midnight, said this morning in Standring Memorial Hospital.

Casey's voice trailed off. His head and body were wrapped in bandages. He is badly burned about the face, head, neck, hands and legs. He has a head injury and a broken collarbone.

The "she" uppermost in Casey's mind is Mary Lou Young, 19, his girl in Chicago.

"I waited 16 months (in Korea) to see her," Casey said through swollen lips. "Now I've got to go in this condition."

Condition Satisfactory

Then as if in despair, young Casey added:

"If I could see her, I could die right now!"

(Doctors at the hospital said Casey, though badly injured and suffering from shock, is considered in satisfactory condition.)

Casey was among the 2,833 passengers who arrived here from the Far East yesterday aboard the Gen. R. L. Howze, the last regular troopship to bring Korean servicemen back home.

By a "streak of luck," Casey related, he sat on the left side of the big plane, near the emergency door.

Casey recalled how the plane's take-off from Boeing Field was delayed. "It stayed there and stayed there and stayed there," he said.

"We got just about here (the crash site) and the whole plane started jarring. I saw wires snap.

He Walked Through Fire

"I don't know how I got out. I walked right through the fire.

"I crawled and the man in front of me was screaming. I was afraid if I fell down I wouldn't be able to go on.

"Some G. I. stumbled down and I grabbed him. He started screaming. I walked and crawled up to the house (of Mr. and Mrs. Charles Platts).

"I didn't think I'd make it. I never screamed or prayed so hard in all my life."

Casey is the son of Mr. and Mrs. J. P. Casey of Chicago.

"I waited so long to go home," Casey repeated. "All I want to see is my girl."

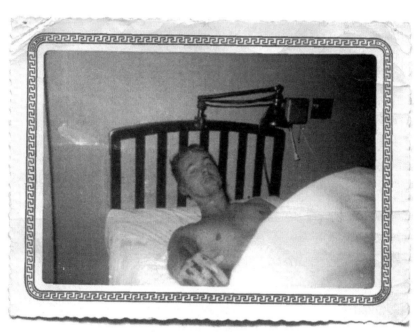

GENE RECOVERING

```
LD52 OF GOVT PD DUPLICATE OF TELEPHONED TELEGRAM
         WUX CHICAGO ILL 341AMC NOV 20 1955
MRS ANNA MARIE CASEY   MAIL COPY
         7757 SOUTH MICHIGAN AVE CHICAGO ILL
FROM AMPCL-RRS-A 11-376 REFERENCE TELEGRAM DATED 18 NOVEMBER
1955 ADVISING YOU OF THE CONDITION OF YOUR SON SP3 EUGENE
CASEY THE FOLLOWING ADDITIONAL INFORMATION IS FURNISHED PD
ATTENDING PHYSICIAN GEORGE L STANDRING MEMORIAL HOSPITAL
STATES TODAY YOUR SON SLIGHTLY IMPROVED FROM YESTERDAY.
     CO RTNRSGSTA 6021SU FTLAWTON WASH 192035Z.
```

SECOND TELEGRAM WITH UPDATE ON GENE'S CONDITION

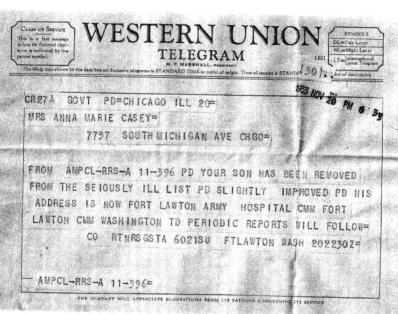

ANOTHER TELEGRAM UPDATING GENE'S FAMILY ON HIS CONDITION

CASEY FAMILY HOME IN CHICAGO

Marriage and Children

The 1950's was under the Cold War umbrella, but many happier events occurred worth noting. The Wham-O Company produced the first Frisbee. Buddy Holly and the Crickets recorded *That'll Be the Day*. Ford Motor Company revealed their luxury car, the Edsel. *American Bandstand*, *Wagon Train*, *Perry Mason*, and *Leave It to Beaver* were some of the many television programs that premiered.

"In 1957, I married Marilyn Charlotte Kohl and we were blessed with four children; Ken in 1958, Keith in 1960, Michael in 1964, and Suzi in 1970. My grandchildren are Jamie, Krystal, Adam, Aaron, and Daniel. Marilyn and I grew up living across the street from each other through most of the '40's. We both attended St. Dorothy's grammar school. She was two years behind me. When she graduated, she attended Mercy High School where her mom and my sister graduated together. We started dating after I came home from Korea in 1956. We were married on October 5, 1957."

"I worked for Coca Cola, then Capital Ambulance. I was part owner of a used car business and owned a wholesale candy route before becoming a Chicago police officer for ten years. After I left the police department in 1972, I opened Coast to Coast hardware store in Wabash, Indiana. I sold the store in 1975 and worked for Prudential Insurance until 1977 when I bought the Lake Parker Motel in Lakeland, Florida, Williams House of Flowers in Lakeland, and

Bloomin' Idiot Florist in Lauderdale Lakes, Florida. In 1979, I sold the motel and during the next ten years, I owned East Pasco Hearing Aid Center and later the Kountry Kitchen convenience store in Cullman, Alabama, which I sold a year later. I founded Touch of Class Dry Cleaners, in Lakeland, Florida. I finished my working life first at the Florida Department of Transportation, then a construction company, and finally a bank. Amen." In 1991, after thirty-four years of marriage Marilyn and I divorced. She later died from Pick's Disease."

"My second marriage to Sharon Huffstickler blessed me with another son, my stepson Michael. He gave us two more grandchildren, Madison and Mason."

GENE IN FRONT OF HIS COAST TO COAST HARDWARE STORE, WABASH, INDIANA, APRIL 1972.

Being a Police Officer

"I would say that the time I spent as a Chicago police officer was the highlight of my working days," Gene said. "I joined the department in 1962 and left in 1972." Gene's brother, John, was also a Chicago police officer from the '30s to 1956. "He worked out of the Carthage Detail at 11th and State Streets'" Gene said. "John was Jersey Joe Walcott's bodyguard." Jersey Joe, whose real name was Arnold Raymond Cream, was a world heavyweight boxing champion. "John was also a bodyguard for professional figure skater and actress Sonja Henie," Gene said. "John died from injuries in a car crash in 1956."

Gene's heroism was appropriately recognized. "I received many department commendations, (1963, 1964, 1967), and honorable mentions generated by letters sent to my commander about my work on the street as a policeman", Gene said proudly. "I thoroughly enjoyed every moment of it. Too many injuries took me off the street and I lost interest. I just didn't like being behind a desk. The desk life was a good life, but boring. I wasn't into *boring*."

Gene survived two serious accidents during his police career. "In the wee hours of the morning I was assisting a motorist in front of the south end of the Soldiers Field parking lot," Gene explained. "I was struck while in the car, pushed about one hundred yards until I crashed into the fence surrounding the Soldiers Field parking lot, where the Chicago Bears play. I was pinned under the dash in a completely totaled squad car. Fortunately, I had no serious injuries."

Gene paused to recall another serious incident. "The other one was when I was removing injured passengers from a wrecked car at Lake Shore Drive and Randolph Street. An intoxicated driver picked me off, flipped me through the air, and I came down belly flat on the hood of his car. When he hit the brakes, he threw me off the hood of his car, bouncing me on my tail bone. I was in the hospital for a couple of weeks, sent home, relapsed, and sent back for another couple of weeks. I was back on my feet in time to work the night of the fire at McCormack Place in January of 1967. I also worked during the riots after Martin Luther King Jr. was assassinated in April of 1968 and a few months later the Democratic Convention. Amen."

One of Chicago's historical fires occurred at McCormick Place Convention Center on January 16, 1967. "It was said at the time if the beams had been wood and not steel, the building would not have collapsed in on itself," Gene said. "The wood beams would have seared from the flames and then repelled further fire damage. When the building remains were finally cleared, I would patrol the structure, driving on the gigantic concrete slab and look at Lake Michigan."

"I do not recall ever meeting anyone who had survived an airplane crash. I knew a neighbor at one time that was the victim of a robbery in Chicago, and while lying in the street on his back; the perpetrator fired six rounds from a .45 caliber pistol into his chest and stomach. That's about the worst. He survived and lives in Florida. I learned that our bodies are pretty tough."

"I never thought that being a police officer as a constant dangerous threat to me," he said. "I loved helping people and enforcing the laws. The kudos I have gotten out of those ten years, in later years, surpasses any negativity of the job if there was any. I guess power may enter as one of the jobs perks."

"In the ten years on the police department, I pretty much worked the jobs I wanted. I walked a beat and worked an accident patrol car on South Lake Shore Drive and the Stevenson Expressway, a radar unit, and the desk in the hit-and-run unit. The injuries made me think about doing something else. I was always plagued by the back injuries I received in the plane crash that the Army refused to acknowledge until the early 2000s."

"In 1991, when Sharon and I got married, I went to work for the Florida Department of Transportation, (FDOT). I did a short stint involving immigration, construction, then back to FDOT, then back to construction, and finally a new bank, Community Southern Bank. In 2004, I had my first hip replacement. I worked full-time for my wife's bank when I had my last back operation, a failed one at that. I never really had a hobby per se, but I was an avid golfer and a darn good tennis player."

"For saving two men in the crash I was to be awarded the Soldiers Medal," he said. Introduced in July 1926 by Congress, the Soldier's Medal is awarded to any person in the armed forces who heroically risks their life in a situation not directly involved in conflict with the enemy. It is the highest honor a soldier can receive for an act of valor in a non-combat situation. However, as it often happens in life, things didn't go smoothly. "Due to the orders being lost in the shuffle of time and a fire that burned my records, I never was awarded the medal I so justly deserved. I have pursued it the past few years, but to no avail. I think that being transferred to BAMC for burn research interrupted and hampered the follow-up paperwork necessary for the award. Other heroes in the accident did receive the Solder's Medal.

Who knows, maybe I'll get lucky or maybe the story itself will be my legacy."

The destruction and loss of his military service records seem to be the main hurdle. Despite many letters to the Department of the Army, a long list of politicians and letters to the President, as of June 2017 Gene has not received the Solders Medal.

Local Traffic Officer Cracks Burglaries, Narcotic Thefts

CONGRATULATIONS CASEY
Police Supt. O. W. Wilson (left) and Robert E. Raleigh, Citizens Traffic Safety Board representative, congratulate Officer Eugene Casey for solving south side burglaries and narcotics thefts by alert observations and detection.

Violation of a one-way street regulation led to the solution of a series of burglaries, narcotic thefts, check forgeries and car thefts, and this month's Traffic Officer of the Month citation for patrolman Eugene Casey, of 12723 Sangamon.

Officer Casey, assigned to one-man squad car patrol In the Third District, curbed the one-way vilolator's car. The driver and the woman passenger fled. Casey radioed for help and when assistance arrived a search was made of the building and the apartment Into which the couple ran.

Stolen goods, narcotics, an automatic pistol and an assortment of wallets were found.

The arrest solved 12 robberies in drug stores where narcotics were taken as well as 75 burglaries and a number of thefts from autos.

Also cleared up was a robbery on the beach at Calumet Park in which the victim's wallet was pilfered of Railway Express checks which had later been forged and cashed.

The grand jury indicted the couple on charges of burglary, armed robbery and receiving stolen property.

The CTSB each month awards a police officer or officers who solve serious crimes as a result of a stop for a traffic violation.

THIS ARTICLE APPEARED IN SEVERAL CHICAGO AREA NEWSPAPERS IN OCTOBER 1963

ONE OF MANY COMMENDATIONS
PRESENTED TO GENE CASEY

**CHICAGO POLICE DEPARTMENT BASEBALL TEAM;
GENE IN FRONT ROW FAR LEFT**

Happily Ever After

Life is change, both bad and good. People constantly enter our lives in a flash of circumstances and decisions. Some stay for a second while others remain for a long time.

"I've been married to Sharon Huffstickler since 1991," Gene said. "I met her at the bank she worked for, Citrus and Chemical Bank, where I conducted my business. She was a customer service representative and the branch manager. I was always delighted to have her wait on me as she was oh so beautiful, cheerful and very pleasant. She was the branch and the whole bank's *Energizer Bunny*. Always upbeat, always the cheerleader, always the source of 'Let's get this done, let's make this happen'." We both could sense that there was a chemistry between us."

Chemistry between two people has a purpose, a connection that can't be easily dismissed.

"On October 1, 1990 at around 9:05 a.m., Sharon came into my dry cleaning business to see what the operation and store looked like, a request I had made to her many times. After the tour, she took me next door to Publix Super Market to buy me coffee. As we walked into the store, she took hold of my hand. We have not let go of each other since."

Gene paused to think about this classic question. "Do I believe in love at first sight?", he said. "Maybe some people don't, but I do. I believe that every now and then, once in a lifetime, you are drawn to someone so deeply that it's like a magnetic pull. That's how it was with Sharon. This is the woman I could and cannot do anything without, who makes even the mundane poignant."

Twenty-five years have passed into forever. "We were married on May 25, 1991 at the gazebo of the Saw Mill", Gene said, "a small restaurant owned by some friends. A good friend who was a public notary performed the service. Our friend, Steve, was playing music. When we walked together to the gazebo, without Sharon's knowledge, I had the lyrics of Juice Newton's song, *The Sweetest Thing*, changed to *The Sweetest Thing I've Ever Known Is Loving Sharon*. We invited only fifty of our closest friends and family and everything was perfect."

It seems most marriages are touched by a few naysayers who tend to inject their doubt. "Some folks were skeptical and said the marriage would never work," Gene said, "mainly because Sharon is twenty years my junior. However, we have definitely fooled them. Has it been perfect? Nothing ever is, but it has been the best ride of our lives and neither of us would change a thing. Our blended family has worked well although it was not always easy in the beginning. Over the years we have gained admiration and love for each other and we enjoy our grandchildren who bring us great joy. We have had an incredible twenty-five years and look forward to our future together."

FLORIDA GOVERNOR RICK SCOTT (LEFT) GREETING GENE AT A CEREMONY HONORING KOREAN WAR VETERANS ON AUGUST 13, 2014 AT THE EISENHOWER RECREATION CENTER IN THE VILLIAGE, FLORIDA.

GENE AND SHARON

Acknowledgements, Credits, and References

All photographs courtesy of Gene Casey except for the following:

Cover photographs by Steve De Roeck, image copyright www.deroeck.uk
 Thank you, Mr. De Roeck.
Chatham Bowling Alley - Photo by J.R. Schmidt.
 Thank you, Mr. Schmidt.

The Seattle Times

Cover design and photograph edits by Gary Moffitt.
 Thank you for the many hours of work you devoted to this project. It means more than I can express.

Air Disaster.com, www.airdisaster.com.
Army.com, www.army.com/info/posts/fort-crowder.
Bearshistory, www.bearshistory.com/source/home.as.
Chicago Tribune.com, www.articles.chicagotribune.com.
Federal Aviation Administration, www.faa.gov.
HistoryOrb, www.historyorb.com/date/1955/november/17.
National Transportation Safety Board, www.ntsb.gov.
Newspaper Archives, www.newspaperarchive.com.

PlaneCrashInfo.com, www.planecrashinfo.com.
Stars and Stripes Digital Archives, www.starsandstripes. newspaperarchive.com.
Timelines of History, www.timelines.ws
Wikipedia, www.wikipedia.org/wiki/Soldier%27s_Medal.

Every effort has been made to ensure the facts and authenticity of the contents of this book are correct.

Made in the USA
Lexington, KY
10 April 2018